Cool Jokes

to make you laugh!

This book belongs to:

MARKS & SPENCER

Cool Jokes

to make you laugh!

Marks and Spencer p.l.c.
PO Box 3339, Chester CH99 9QS
www.marksandspencer.com

This book was created by Magpie Books, an imprint of Constable & Robinson Ltd

Inside illustrations courtesy of Mike Phillips

A copy of the British Library Cataloguing-in-Publication Data is available from the British Library

Printed in China

ISBN 1-84461-435-2

Contents:

Arctic Howlers

What is a woolly mammoth's favourite sport?

Squash.

What's huge and hairy and goes up and down?

A woolly mammoth in a lift.

Why do woolly mammoths lie on their backs with their legs in the air?

To trip up birds.

How do you make a waterfall?

Throw a bucket of water out of the window.

What do you get when a woolly mammoth sky dives?

A large hole.

How do you know when there's a blue whale in your cupboard?

You can't shut the door.

What looks exactly like a woolly mammoth, but weighs nothing?

A woolly mammoth's shadow.

Why did the polar bear eat a clock?

He was just killing time.

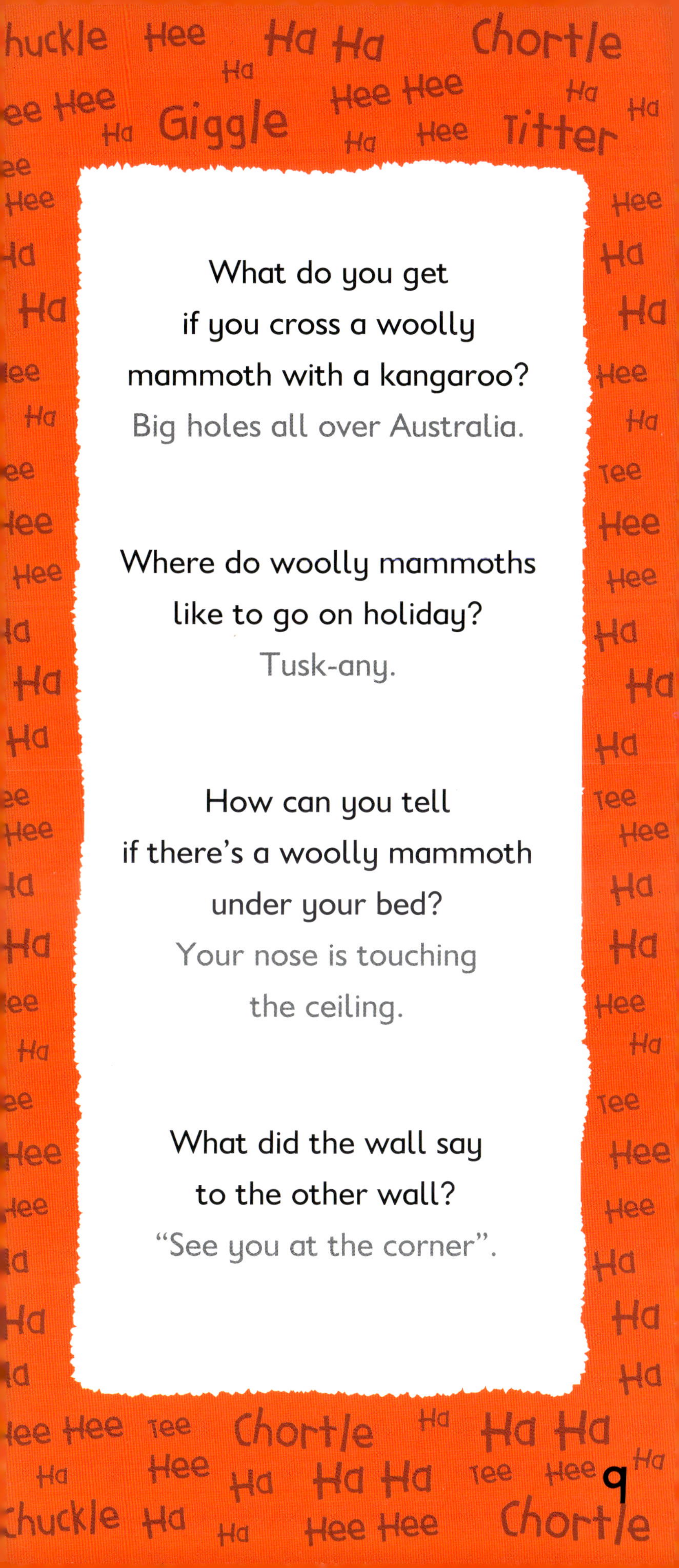

What do you get
if you cross a woolly
mammoth with a kangaroo?
Big holes all over Australia.

Where do woolly mammoths
like to go on holiday?
Tusk-any.

How can you tell
if there's a woolly mammoth
under your bed?
Your nose is touching
the ceiling.

What did the wall say
to the other wall?
"See you at the corner".

Why did the woolly mammoth eat the stupid man?

Because someone said he was nuts.

How do you get down from a woolly mammoth?

You don't get down from woolly mammoths; you get down from ducks.

How many polar bears can dance on the head of a pin?

None, polar bears can't dance.

Why did the bee fly with his legs crossed?

To get to the BP station.

Why do woolly mammoths paint their toenails?

So they can hide in packets of jelly beans.

Why can't woolly mammoths ride bicycles?

Because they don't have thumbs to ring the bell.

Why was the woolly mammoth red?

You would be too if you had so many jokes told about you.

What did the cavemen do when they saw a woolly mammoth running down the path?

They ran.

What kind of eggs does an evil chicken lay?

Devilled.

What game do fish like playing the most?

Name that tuna.

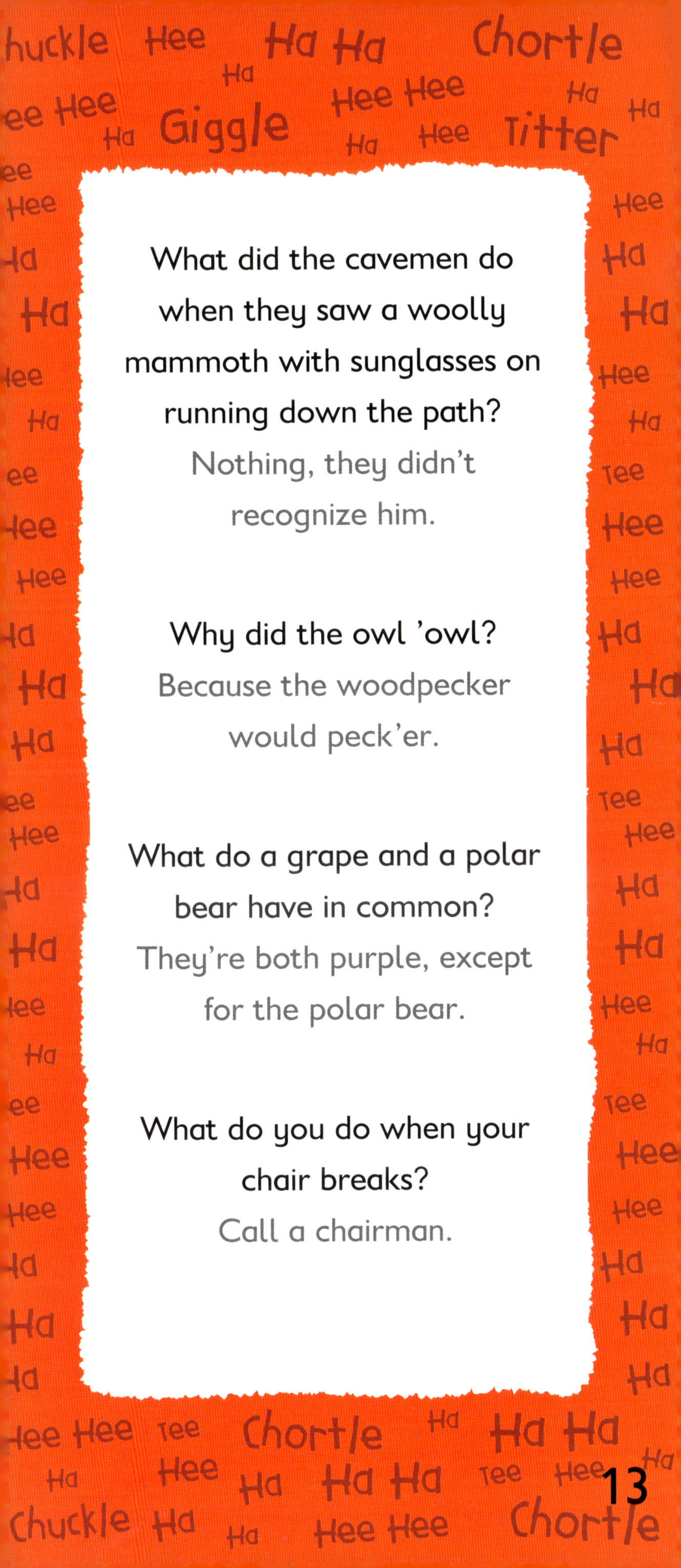

What did the cavemen do when they saw a woolly mammoth with sunglasses on running down the path?
Nothing, they didn't recognize him.

Why did the owl 'owl?
Because the woodpecker would peck'er.

What do a grape and a polar bear have in common?
They're both purple, except for the polar bear.

What do you do when your chair breaks?
Call a chairman.

How do you fit
a sabre-toothed tiger
into a matchbox?
Take out the woolly
mammoth.

Why don't woolly
mammoths like to go
swimming?
Because it's hard to keep
their trunks up.

What do you get
if you cross a jaguar
with a woolly mammoth?
A car with a big trunk.

How do you make a woolly mammoth float?

Add a woolly mammoth to two scoops of vanilla ice cream and some milk.

What is huge, hairy and has sixteen wheels?

A woolly mammoth on roller skates.

Why did the reindeer paint his toenails red?
So he could hide in the cherry tree.

Why is a snail stronger than a woolly mammoth?
A snail carries its house, but a woolly mammoth only carries a trunk.

What happened to Ray when a woolly mammoth stepped on him?
He became an X-Ray.

Who sleeps at the bottom of the sea?
Jack the kipper.

Why did the twin woolly mammoths get kicked off the beach?
Because they only had one pair of trunks between them.

What time is it when a yeti sits on your fence?
Time to fix the fence.

Why did the snowman stand on the marshmallow?
So he wouldn't fall in the hot chocolate.

What is a dolphin's favourite TV show?
Whale of fortune.

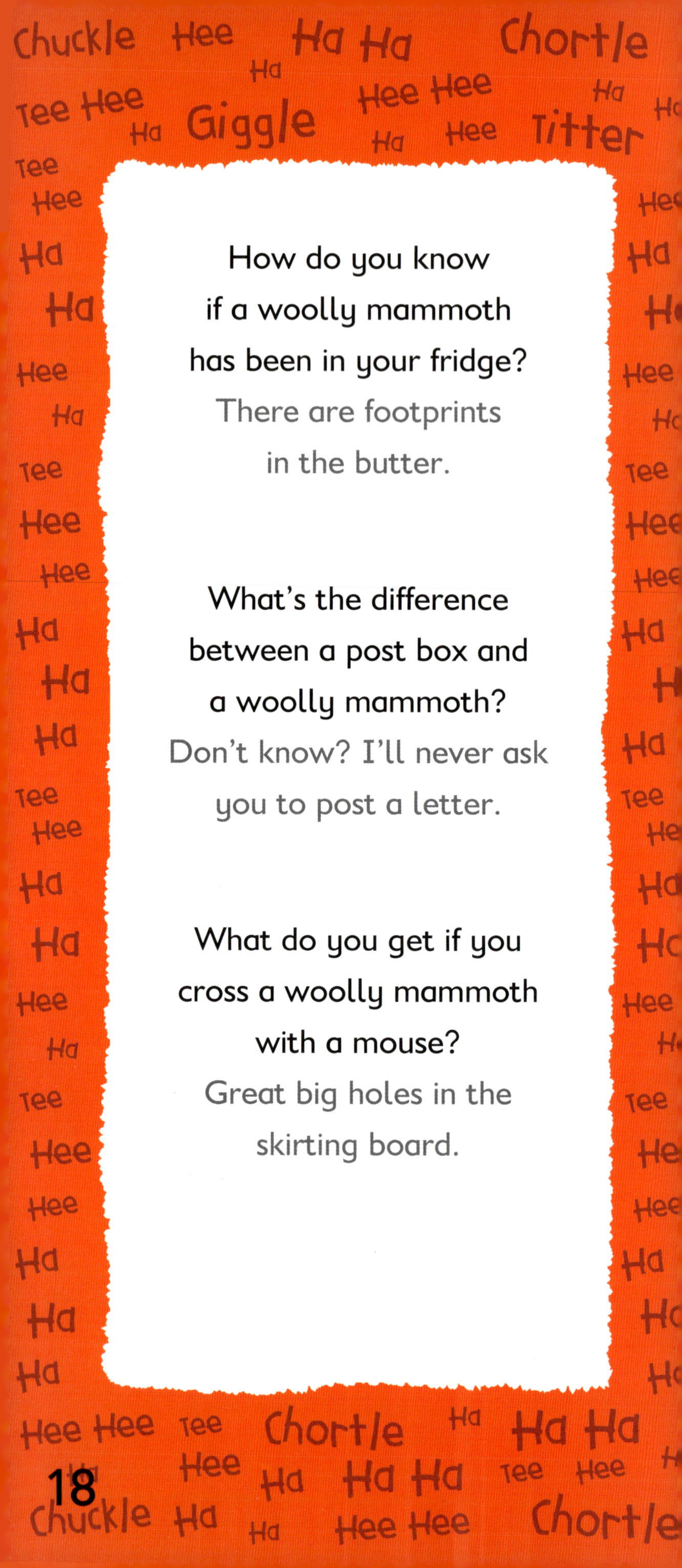

How do you know if a woolly mammoth has been in your fridge?
There are footprints in the butter.

What's the difference between a post box and a woolly mammoth?
Don't know? I'll never ask you to post a letter.

What do you get if you cross a woolly mammoth with a mouse?
Great big holes in the skirting board.

How does a walrus
get up a tree?
He sits on an acorn
and waits for it to grow.

How does a walrus
get out of a tree?
He sits on a leaf
and waits for autumn.

What's the difference
between woolly mammoths
and elephants?
Elephants don't need
to carry combs.

Did you hear about the fish
that went deaf?
He had to buy a herring aid.

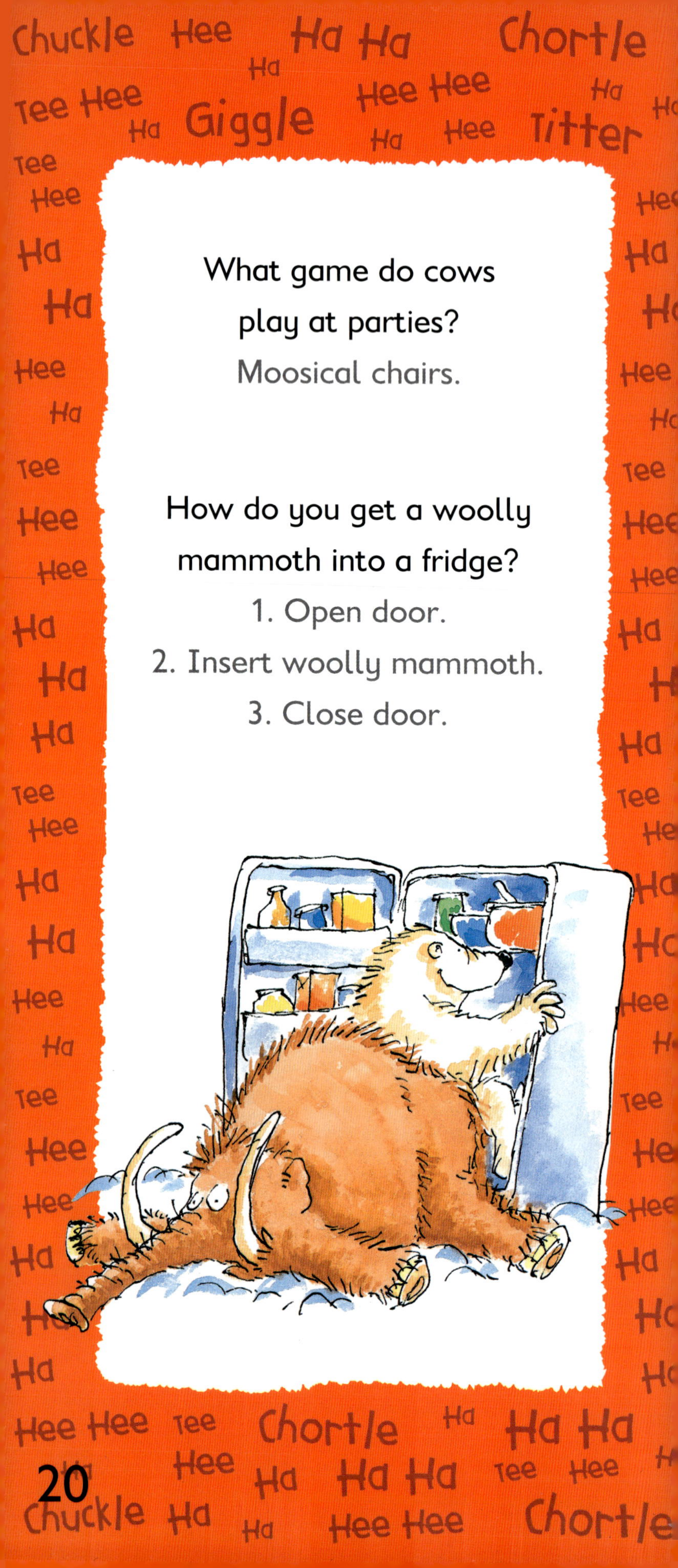

What game do cows play at parties?

Moosical chairs.

How do you get a woolly mammoth into a fridge?

1. Open door.
2. Insert woolly mammoth.
3. Close door.

How do you get
a polar bear into a fridge?
1. Open door.
2. Remove woolly mammoth.
3. Insert polar bear.
4. Close door.

How do you get a woolly mammoth out of a fridge?
Tell him it's cooler in the freezer.

What is the difference between a penguin and a grape?
Penguins don't have pips.

How do you get
four woolly mammoths
into a mini?
Two in the front,
two in the back.

What did the fifth woolly
mammoth in the
mini discover?
The sunroof.

How do you know
there are three woolly
mammoths in your fridge?
There'll be one waiting
outside in the mini.

What is a husky dog's
favourite sport?
Formula 1 drooling.

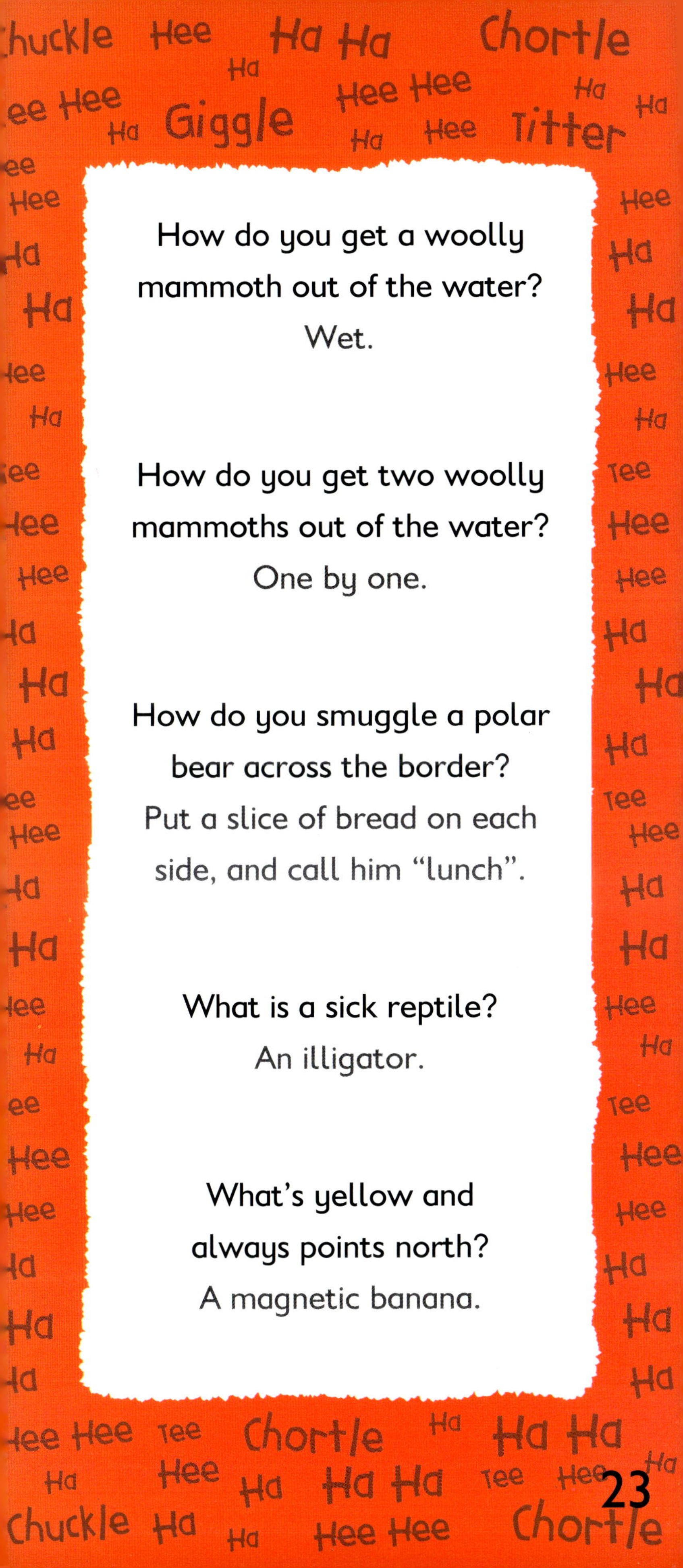

How do you get a woolly mammoth out of the water?
Wet.

How do you get two woolly mammoths out of the water?
One by one.

How do you smuggle a polar bear across the border?
Put a slice of bread on each side, and call him "lunch".

What is a sick reptile?
An illigator.

What's yellow and always points north?
A magnetic banana.

Why are woolly
mammoths woolly?
Because silk is too expensive.

Why are woolly
mammoths wrinkled?
Because they sit
in the bath too long.

Where had the runner been?
To see the celery stalk.

What moves around
a bus at 1,000 mph?
A lightning conductor.

Why did the sea-lion
fall out of the tree?
Because it was dead.

Why did the second sea-lion
fall out of the tree?
It was glued to the first one.

Why did the third sea-lion
fall out of the tree?
It thought it was a game.

Why did the tree fall down?
It thought it was a sea-lion.

What do you get
if you cross a spider
with a woolly mammoth?
I don't know, but if it
crawls on the ceiling your
roof will collapse.

What do you do when a woolly mammoth stubs his toe?

Call a toe truck.

How do you shoot a blue woolly mammoth?

With a blue woolly mammoth gun, of course.

What do you call two woolly mammoths on a bicycle?

Optimistic.

What do you call a musical insect?

A humbug.

What was the woolly mammoth doing on the motorway?

About five miles per hour.

Why were there so many woolly mammoths running around in the Stone Age?

Because cavemen didn't have fridges.

Why are polar bears' feet shaped the way they are?
To fit on lily pads.

Why isn't it safe to walk on lily pads between two and four in the afternoon?
That's when the polar bears are walking on the lily pads.

Why are frogs so short?
They walk on lily pads between two and four in the afternoon.

What's green, curly and religious?
Lettuce pray.

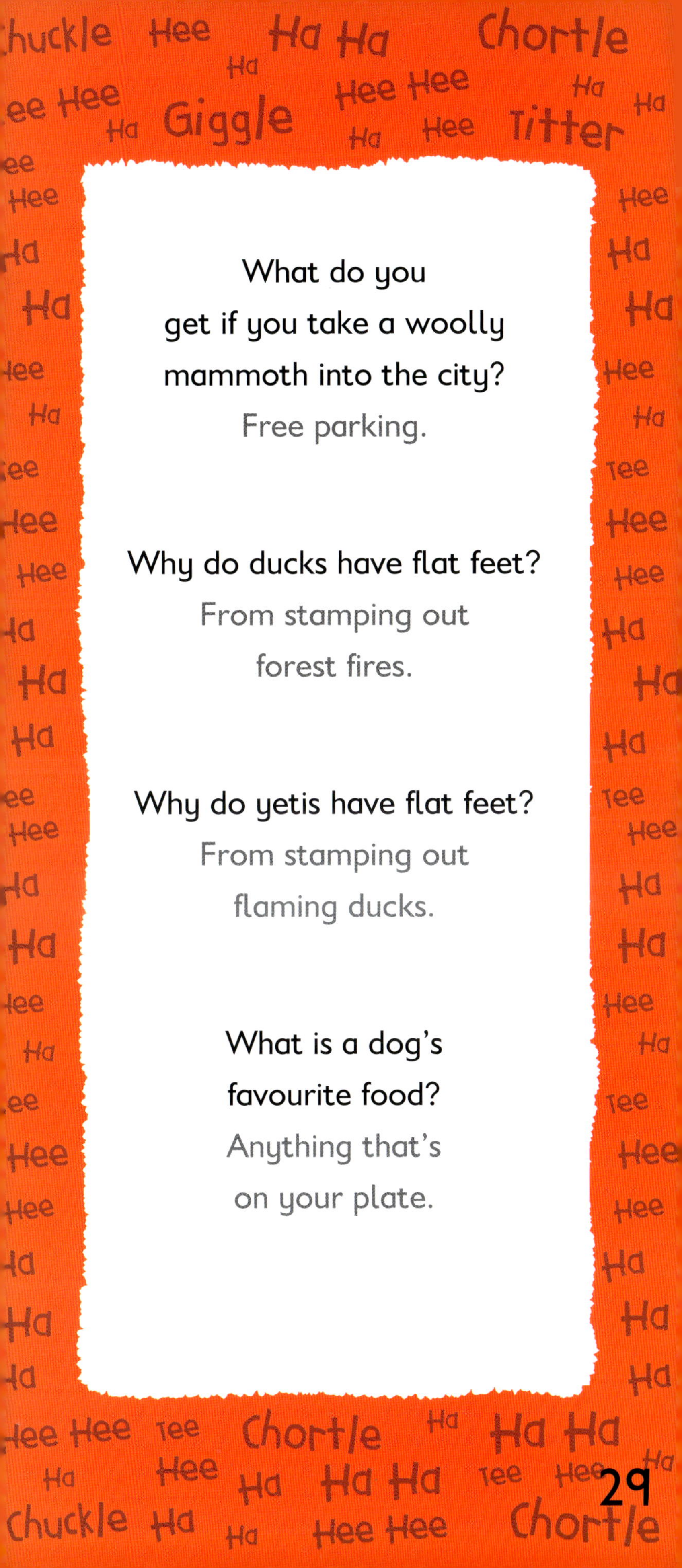

What do you get if you take a woolly mammoth into the city?

Free parking.

Why do ducks have flat feet?

From stamping out forest fires.

Why do yetis have flat feet?

From stamping out flaming ducks.

What is a dog's favourite food?

Anything that's on your plate.

What does it tell you when you see three polar bears walking down the street wearing blue sweatshirts?

They're all on the same team.

How do you know if there's a woolly mammoth in your bed?

All the bed clothes are taken.

Why do woolly mammoths have trunks?

Because they would look silly with glove compartments.

What do you get when you cross an ant with a yeti?

A dead ant.

How many woolly mammoths does it take to screw in a light bulb?

Two, but you need a really big light bulb.

What has two tails, two trunks, five feet and a wig?

A woolly mammoth with spare parts.

Where are most fish found?

Between the head and the tail.

What is more difficult than getting a woolly mammoth into the back seat of your car?
Getting two woolly mammoths into the back seat of your car.

What do you call a fly with no wings?
A walk.

How many woolly mammoths can you fit into a hatchback?
Five — two in the front, two in the back and one in the glove compartment.

Why didn't the penguin do well at school?
All his marks were below "c" level.

How do you catch a squirrel?
Climb into a tree and act like a nut.

Why don't cannibals eat comedians?

Because they taste funny.

What did the dog say to the tree?

"Bark."

What do you call a missing parrot?

A polygon.

How long does it take to learn to skate?

About a dozen sittings.

When is a car not a car?

When it turns into a driveway.

What's the difference between a mosquito and a fly?
A mosquito can fly, but a fly can't mosquito.

What do you call a sleeping cow?
A bulldozer.

Did you know that five out of three people have trouble with fractions?

Why is it not safe to sleep on trains?
Because they run over sleepers.

Ice Breakers

What did the sea say to the iceberg?
Nothing, it just waved.

What's grey, eats fish and lives in Washington DC?
The presidential seal.

Where do penguins go to dance?
The snow ball.

What creature can fly underwater?
A fly in a submarine.

Why are penguins popular on the Internet?
Because they have web feet.

How do penguins drink?
Out of beak-ers.

What's a penguin's favourite salad?
Iceberg lettuce.

When are eyes not eyes?
When a cold wind makes them water.

What's the coldest creature in the sea?
A blue whale.

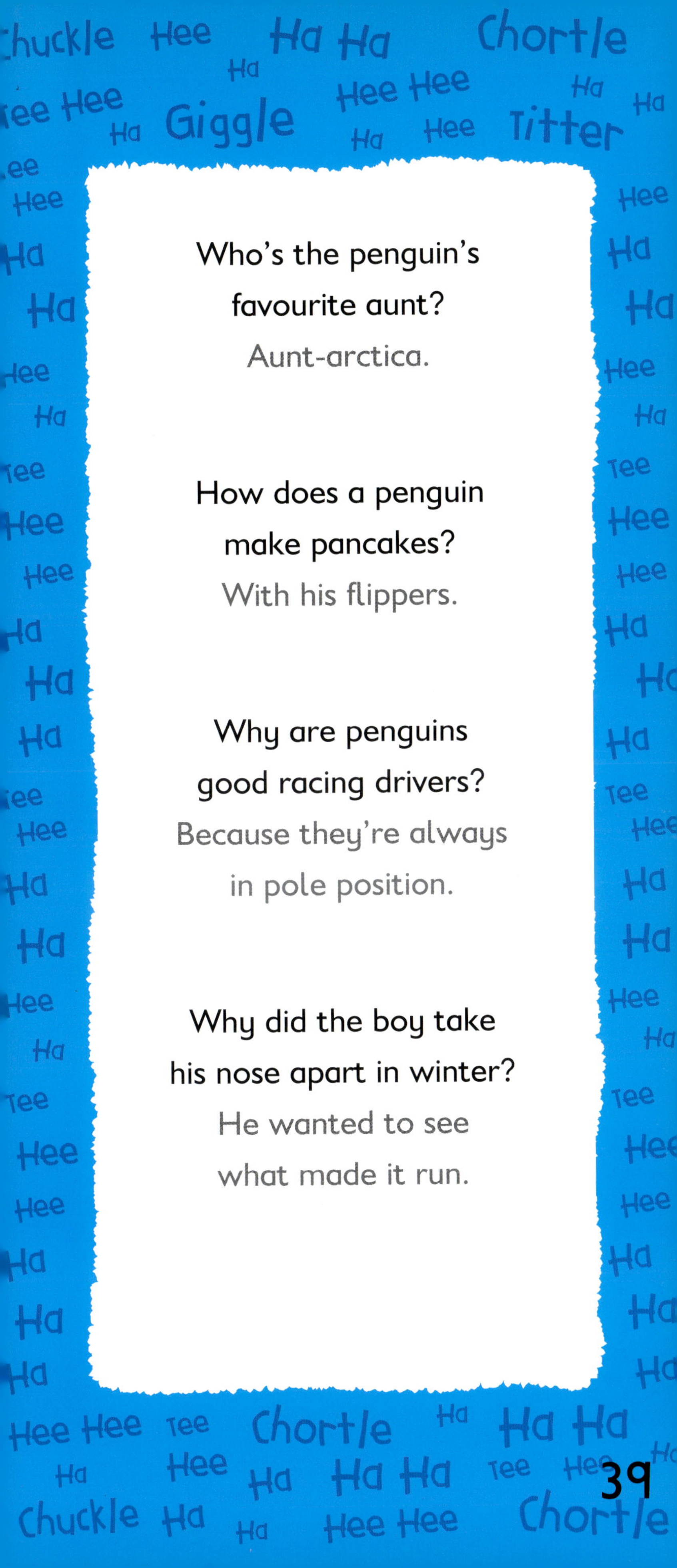

Who's the penguin's favourite aunt?

Aunt-arctica.

How does a penguin make pancakes?

With his flippers.

Why are penguins good racing drivers?

Because they're always in pole position.

Why did the boy take his nose apart in winter?

He wanted to see what made it run.

Where do penguins keep their money?
In the snow bank.

What do you get if you cross an elephant with the Abominable Snowman?
A jumbo yeti.

Why was the pelican kicked out of the hotel?
Because he had a big bill.

Where does money fall like snow?
Wherever there's a change in the weather.

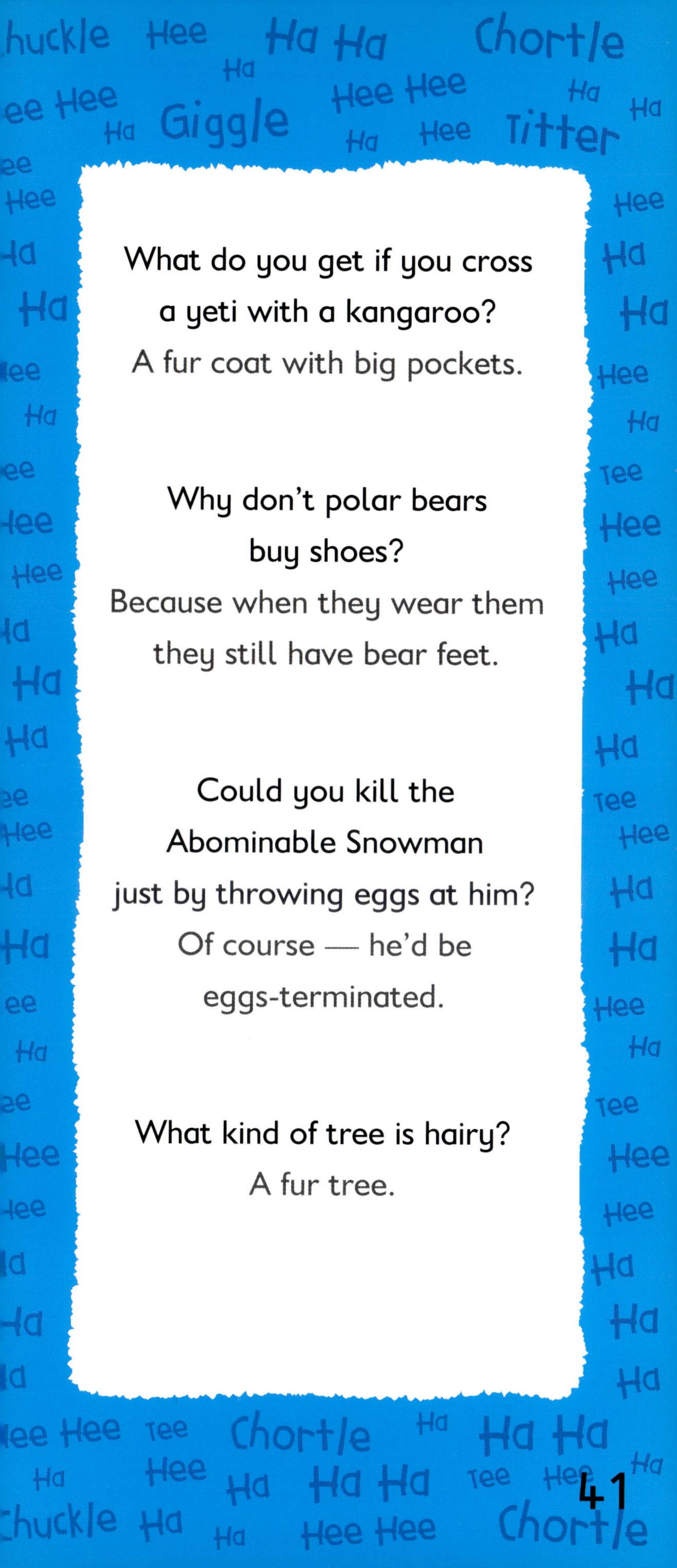

What do you get if you cross a yeti with a kangaroo?

A fur coat with big pockets.

Why don't polar bears buy shoes?

Because when they wear them they still have bear feet.

Could you kill the Abominable Snowman just by throwing eggs at him?

Of course — he'd be eggs-terminated.

What kind of tree is hairy?

A fur tree.

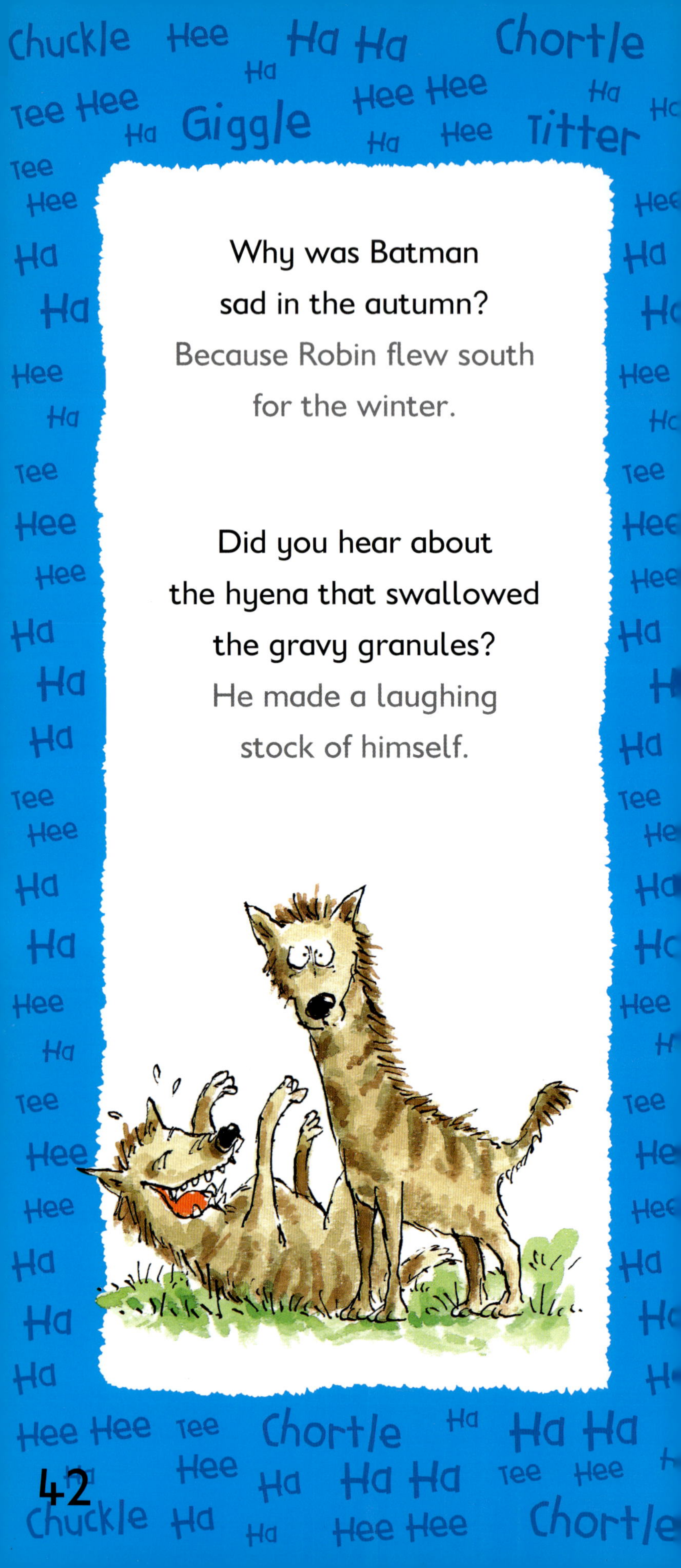

Why was Batman sad in the autumn?
Because Robin flew south for the winter.

Did you hear about the hyena that swallowed the gravy granules?
He made a laughing stock of himself.

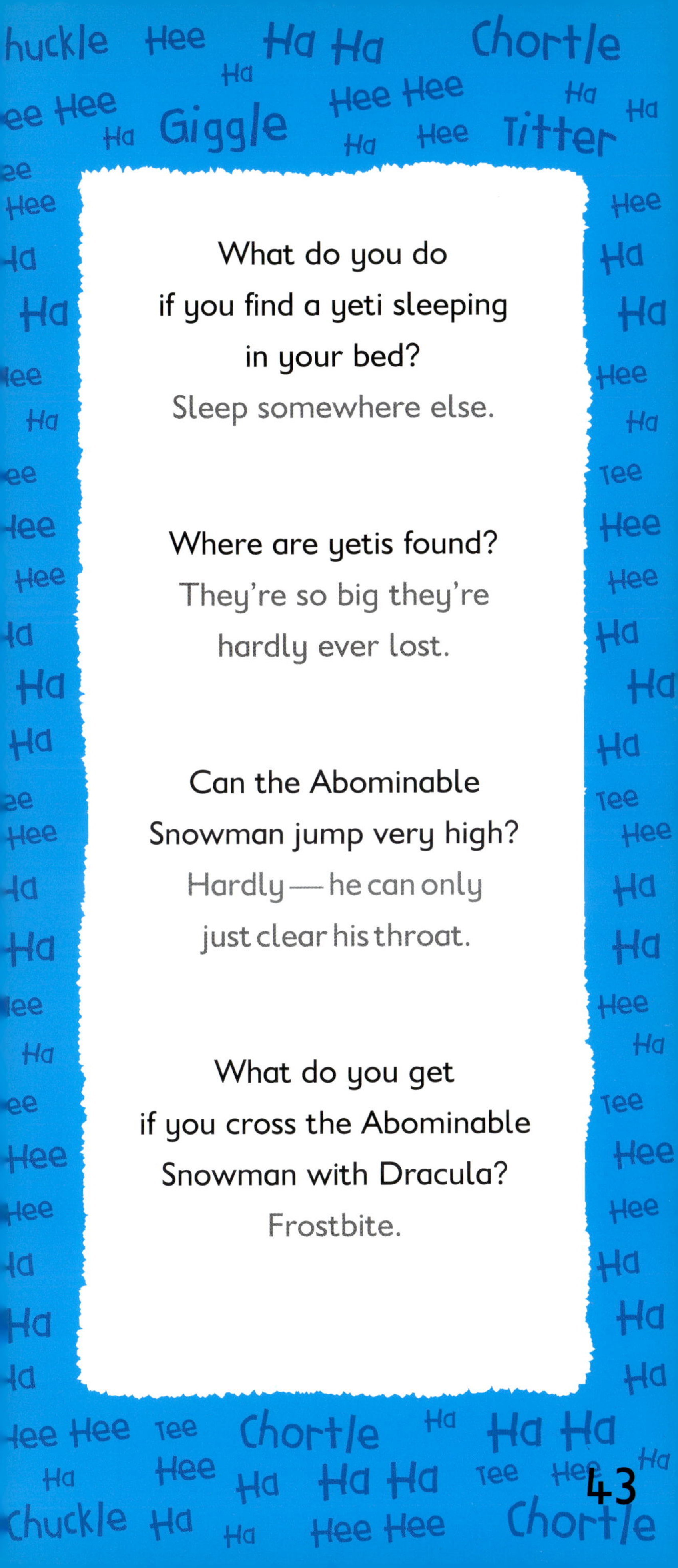

What do you do
if you find a yeti sleeping
in your bed?
Sleep somewhere else.

Where are yetis found?
They're so big they're
hardly ever lost.

Can the Abominable
Snowman jump very high?
Hardly — he can only
just clear his throat.

What do you get
if you cross the Abominable
Snowman with Dracula?
Frostbite.

What kind of man doesn't like to sit in front of the fire?
The Abominable Snowman.

What is the Abominable Snowman's favourite book?
War and Frozen Peas.

What did the Abominable Snowman do after he had his teeth pulled out?
He ate the dentist.

Why was the bird arrested?
Because he was a robin.

What happened to the cold jellyfish?
It set.

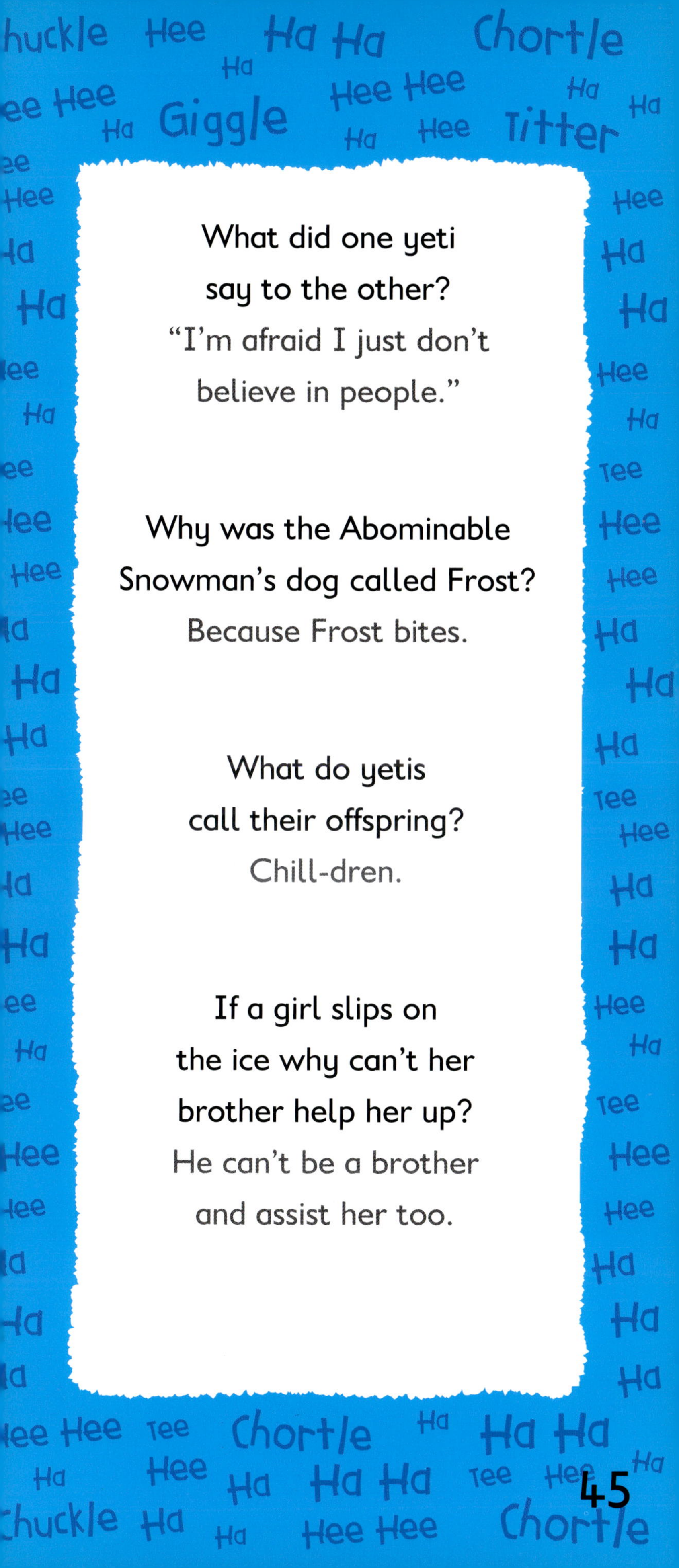

What did one yeti
say to the other?
"I'm afraid I just don't
believe in people."

Why was the Abominable
Snowman's dog called Frost?
Because Frost bites.

What do yetis
call their offspring?
Chill-dren.

If a girl slips on
the ice why can't her
brother help her up?
He can't be a brother
and assist her too.

Why did the Abominable Snowman send his father to Siberia?
Because he wanted frozen pop.

Did you hear the joke about the fierce yeti?
It'll make you roar.

Why do cows wear bells?
Because their horns don't work.

What did the stag say to her children?
"Hurry up, deers!"

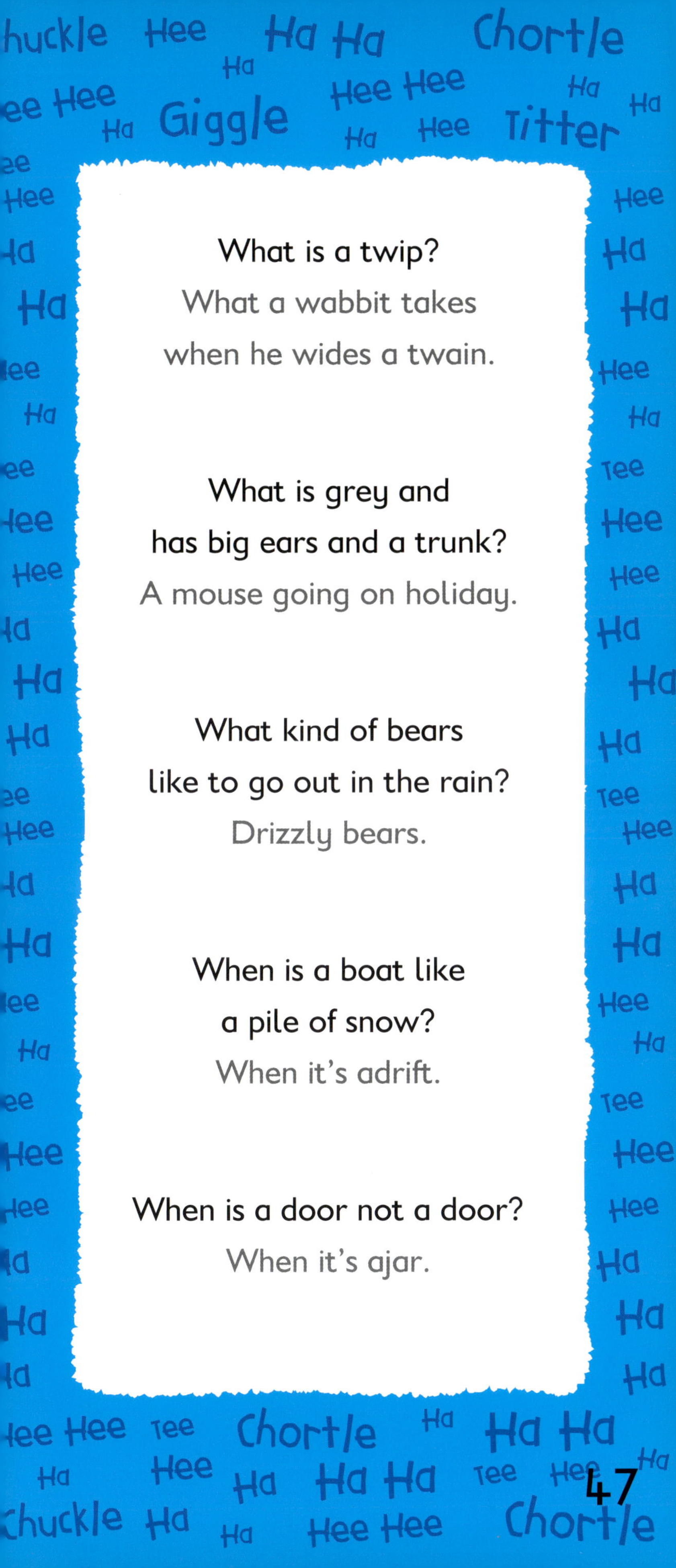

What is a twip?
What a wabbit takes
when he wides a twain.

What is grey and
has big ears and a trunk?
A mouse going on holiday.

What kind of bears
like to go out in the rain?
Drizzly bears.

When is a boat like
a pile of snow?
When it's adrift.

When is a door not a door?
When it's ajar.

What did the mayonnaise say to the fridge?

"Would you mind closing the door, I'm dressing."

Where do fish wash?

In a river basin.

Why did the penguin cross the road?

To go with the floe.

What do penguins take to school?
Ice-pack lunch.

Why don't penguins carry fish in their pockets?
Because they don't have pockets.

Why do penguins carry fish in their beaks?
I told you — because they don't have pockets.

Who has large antlers and wears white gloves?
Mickey Moose.

What did the snowball
do when it stopped rolling?
Looked round.

How do you stop
a dog barking in the
back seat of a car?
Put him in the front seat.

What side of a turkey
do the feathers grow on?
The outside.

When is the Arctic Ocean
like a piece of string?
When a ship makes
knots in it.

What's the difference between a dog and a painter?

One sheds his coat and the other coats his shed.

What did the scientist say when he found bones on the moon?

"The cow didn't make it."

Why can't a leopard hide?

Because he's always spotted.

Where are there no fat people?

In Finland.

What do little penguins sing when their father brings fish home for dinner?

"Freeze a jolly good fellow."

What do you call a man who floats across an ocean?

Bob.

What do you call a gigantic polar bear?

Nothing, you just run away.

What happens to a reindeer when it stands out in the rain?

It gets wet.

What do you get if you cross a woolly mammoth with a whale?

A submarine with a built-in snorkel.

What's black white black white black white black white black white?

A penguin rolling down stairs.

What do cows do on
Saturday nights?
Go to the mooooooovies.

What's black and white,
lives in the Antartic and
is highly dangerous?
A penguin with
a machine gun.

What kind of dog
tells the time?
A watchdog.

What do you use to cut
through giant waves?
A sea-saw.

What do you
call a hundred bunnies
jumping backwards?
A receding hair-line.

What do you call a monkey
holding a firecracker?
A baboom.

How do you stop
a rhino from charging?
Take away its credit card.

What's big, black
and eats polar bears?
A big, black polar bear-eater.

Why shouldn't you dance with a yeti?

Because you might get flat feet.

What's very fat, very ugly and loves fetching sticks?

Jabba the Mutt.

What do you call a yeti
in a phone box?
Stuck.

How did the yeti feel
when he had flu?
Abominable.

What do yetis eat
on top of Everest?
High tea.

What animal talks too much?
A yak.

What do you call
prehistoric ship disasters?
Tyrannosaurus wrecks.

What kind of car does a cat drive?

A Cat-a-lac.

What's the difference between a piano and a fish?

You can tune a piano, but you can't tuna fish.

What do sharks eat with their peanut butter?

Jellyfish.

Why were the woolly mammoths the last to leave Noah's ark?

They had to pack their trunks.

What did the boy octopus say to the girl octopus?

I want to hold your hand, hand, hand, hand, hand, hand, hand, hand.

What do you do with a blue whale?

Put him by the fire to warm him up.

How do you communicate with a fish?

Drop it a line.

What fish is good for pudding?

A jellyfish.

Where do sheep go to get haircuts?
To the baa baa's shop.

What do cats eat for breakfast?
Mice Crispies.

What do you get if you cross a duck with a rooster?
A bird that wakes you up at the quack of dawn.

What happens to a penguin before it grows up?
It grows down.

What is a slug?

A snail with a housing problem.

What has a head like a dog, a tail like a dog and paws like a dog but isn't a dog?

A puppy.

How does a dog stop a video recorder?

He presses the paws button.

What part of a fish weighs the most?

The scales.

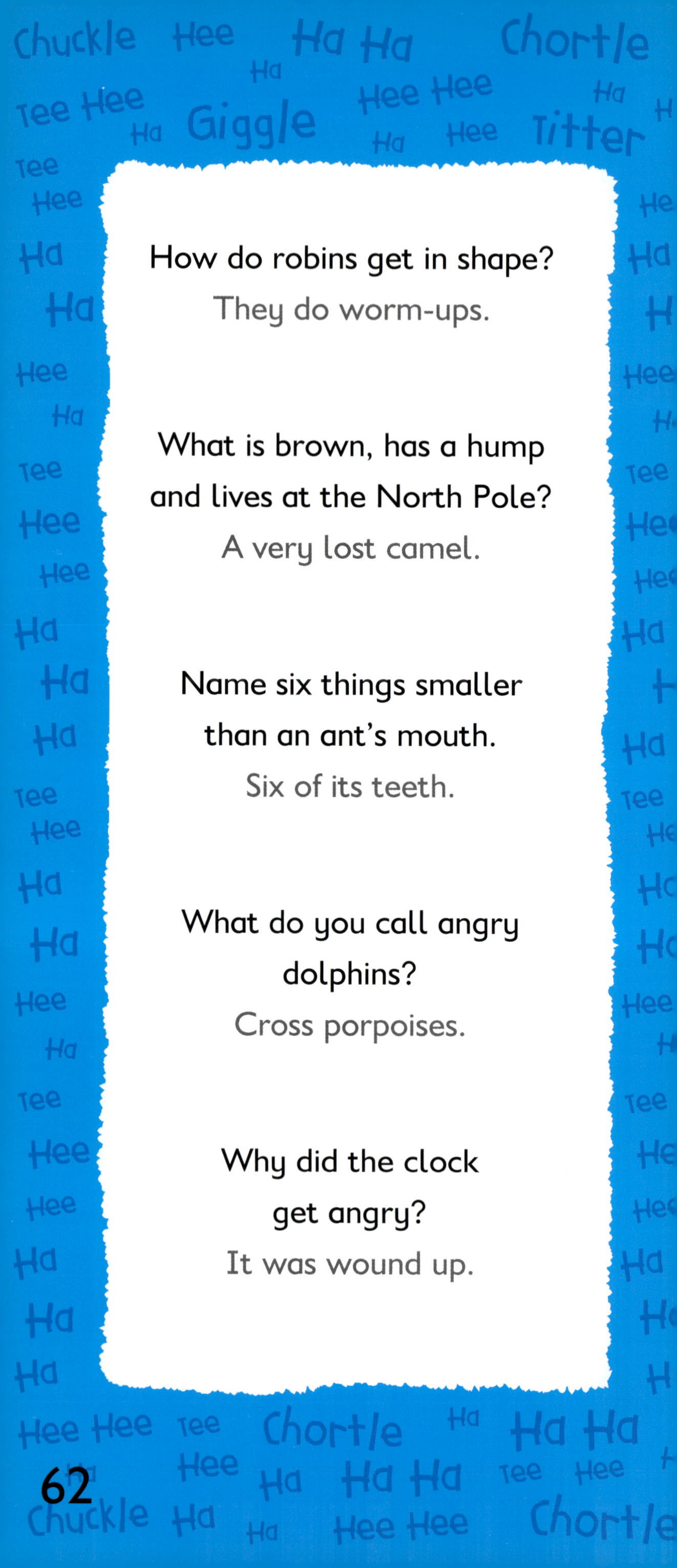

How do robins get in shape?

They do worm-ups.

What is brown, has a hump and lives at the North Pole?

A very lost camel.

Name six things smaller than an ant's mouth.

Six of its teeth.

What do you call angry dolphins?

Cross porpoises.

Why did the clock get angry?

It was wound up.

Did you hear about the cat that swallowed a ball of yarn?

She had mittens.

Why can't skeletons play music in church?

They have no organs.

Where do horses go when they are sick?

To the horsepital.

What happens when a tap, a dog and a tomato run a race?

Well, the dog is in the lead, the tap is running and the tomato is trying to catch up.

Why can't Cinderella play football?

Because she always runs away from the ball.

Where do monkeys make toast?

Under a gorilla.

What do you get if you cross a Mars bar with an elk?

A chocolate mousse.

What do you get
if you sit under a cow?
A pat on the head.

Why did the chicken
cross the playground?
To get to the other slide.

What did one firefly
say to the other when
his light went out?
"Give me a push,
my battery is dead."

What sort of drink
would you get from
a polar bear?
Iced tea.

What did the bald man say when he got a comb for his birthday?

"Thanks, I'll never part with it."

What do you give a seasick yeti?

Plenty of room.

What do you call a box of fifty ducks?

A box of quackers.

What do you call
a pony with a sore throat?
A little hoarse.

What mouse
doesn't eat cheese?
A computer mouse.

How do rabbits send letters?
By haremail.

When is a painting like
a tin of sardines?
When it's done in oils.

What do rabbits
do when they get married?
Go on a bunnymoon.

Polar Punchlines

What noise
wakes up penguins?
The crack of dawn.

Why did the snowman
die with his boots on?
Because he didn't want
to stub his toe when
he kicked the bucket.

What do you get if you cross
a polar bear with a flower?
I don't know, but I'm not
going to smell it.

Who is a husky dog's
favourite comedian?
Growlcho Marx.

Why did Father Christmas take a pencil to bed?

To draw the curtains.

What do you call a mammoth wearing five balaclavas and a big furry hat?

Anything you like — he can't hear you.

Why did the policeman call his dog Camera?

Because it was always snapping.

What happened when the husky dog went to the flea circus?

He stole the show.

Would you rather a polar bear ate you or a penguin?

I'd rather the polar bear ate the penguin.

What does Cinderella Seal wear?

Glass flippers.

What's an ig?

An icy house without a toilet.

How can you tell if you have a stupid husky dog?

It chases parked sledges.

What do you call a cow that has just had a baby?

Decalfinated.

What do footballers drink?

Penaltea.

"Doctor, Doctor!
I think I've swallowed
a ten pound note."

"Come back tomorrow
and we'll see if there's
any change."

What is yellow and
very dangerous?

Shark-infested custard.

Where do tough chickens come from?

Hard-boiled eggs.

What do you call a camel with no humps?

Humphrey.

What says “quick, quick”?

A duck with hiccups.

How do mountains hear?

They have mountaineers.

What kind of coat can you put on when it’s wet?

A coat of paint.

There's an igloo made of ice,
it has ice chairs, ice floors
and ice walls, an ice door
and an ice roof.
What are the stairs made of?
Igloos don't have stairs.

What do you get if you cross
a teddy bear with a pig?
A teddy boar.

What should you call
a bald teddy?
Fred bear.

Where are husky
dogs trained?
In mush rooms.

What steps would you take if an angry polar bear came rushing towards you?

Great big ones.

What animal do you look like when you get into the bath?

A little bear.

Why is a polar bear cheap to have as a pet?

It lives on ice.

Who ate his animals two by two?

Noah Shark.

How do you know which end of a worm is its head?
Tickle it and see which end laughs.

What did one candle say to the other candle?
"Shall we go out tonight?"

On a cold winter's day what are you likely to see close at hand?
A glove.

How do you get six donkeys in a fire engine?
Two in the front, two in the back and two on the top shouting "Eeyore, eeyore, eeyore".

What do you get
when you cross a camera
with a crocodile?
A snap shot.

What do you call
a man with a car
on his head?
Jack.

What's the fastest
cake in the world?
Scone.

What kind of money
do polar bears use?
Ice lolly.

What do you call
a big white bear with
a hole in his middle?
A polo bear.

Why do polar bears
like bald men?
Because they have a great,
white, bear place.

What is the difference
between Father Christmas
and a warm dog?
Father Christmas wears a
whole suit, a dog just pants.

Why was the little bear so spoiled?

Because its mother panda'd to its every whim.

How do you start a teddy bear race?

Ready, teddy, go.

What is huge, white and furry but invisible?

No polar bears.

Why don't husky dogs make good dancers?

Because they have two left feet.

What do Attila the Hun
and Winnie the Pooh
have in common?
They both have "the"
as their middle names.

What do polar bears
have for lunch?
Ice burgers.

What do you get if you cross
a polar bear and a harp?
A bear-faced lyre.

What do you do if your
husky dog eats your pen?
Use a pencil instead.

What's yellow,
comes from Peru and is
completely unknown?
Waterloo Bear, Paddington
Bear's forgotten cousin.

What do you get if you cross
a skunk with a bear?
Winnie the Pooh.

What do you do with two
pieces of bread in the desert?
Make a sandwich.

What's a husky dog's
favourite hobby?
Collecting fleas.

How does an octopus
go to war?
Fully-armed.

What did the zero
say to the eight?
"Nice belt."

What do you get if you cross
a cat with a parrot?
A carrot.

How do we know that carrots are good for your eyesight?
Have you ever seen a rabbit wearing glasses?

What's black and white and read all over?
A newspaper.

What would you do if you broke your leg in two places?
Stay away from those places in future.

What did the traffic light say to the car?
"Don't look now, I'm changing."

Why did the child study in an aeroplane?

He wanted higher education.

Why was the broom late?

It over swept.

Do you know the time?

No, we haven't met yet.

What do you get if you cross a husky dog and a lion?

A terrified postman.

Where did the policeman live?

Nine-nine-nine, Letsbe Avenue.

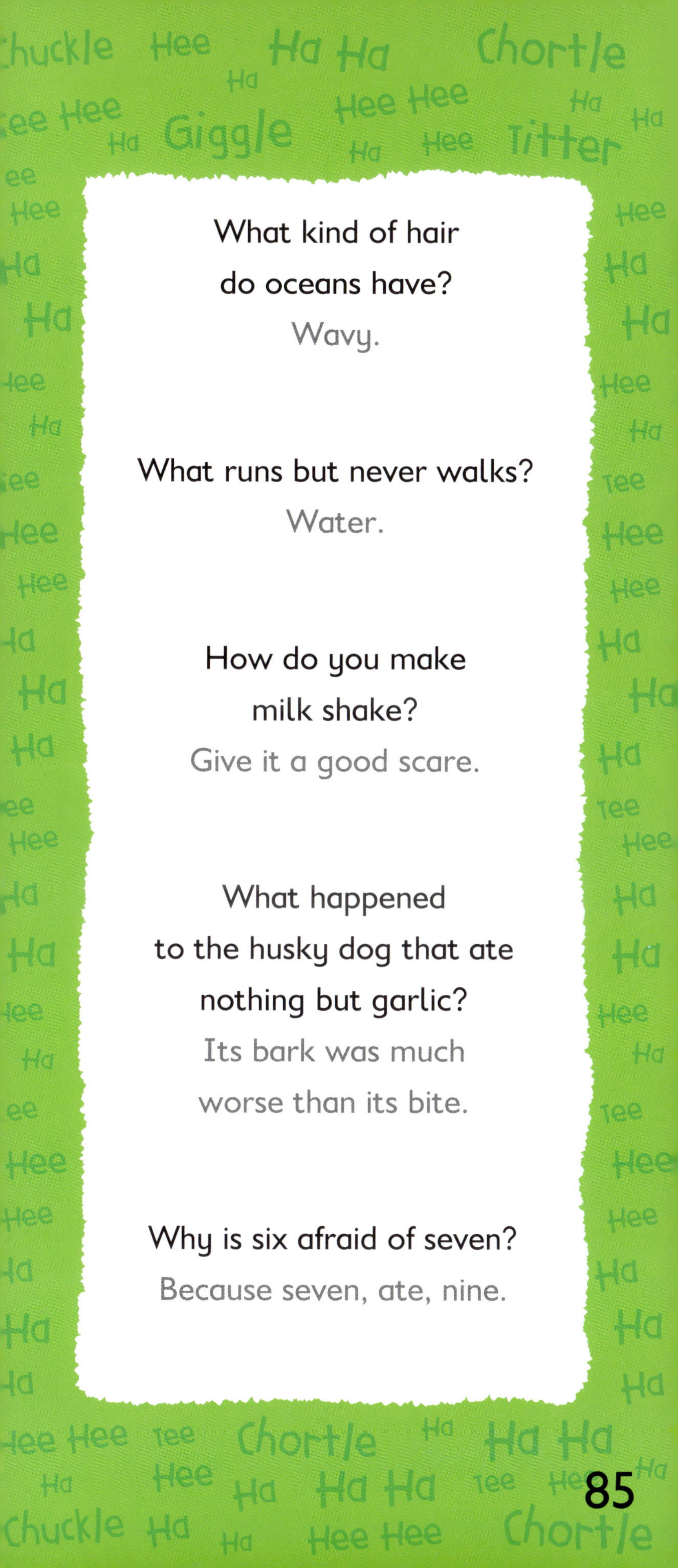

What kind of hair do oceans have?

Wavy.

What runs but never walks?

Water.

How do you make milk shake?

Give it a good scare.

What happened to the husky dog that ate nothing but garlic?

Its bark was much worse than its bite.

Why is six afraid of seven?

Because seven, ate, nine.

Why was the seal swimming backstroke?
It had just had lunch and didn't want to swim on a full stomach.

How do you stop a cold getting to your chest?
Tie a knot in your neck.

What lies at the bottom of the Arctic Sea and shivers?
A nervous wreck.

Why didn't the husky dog speak to his foot?
Because it's not polite to talk back to your paw.

A man was driving a black car, his lights were off, the moon wasn't out, a woman crossed the road in front of him. How did he see her?

It was the middle of the day.

Have you ever seen a man-eating polar bear?

No, but in a café I once saw a man eating chicken.

What do you call a pig that knows karate?

A pork-chop.

Why do mother kangeroos hate rainy days?

Because the kids have to play inside.

What kind of dog can jump higher than a building?

Any dog — buildings can't jump.

What does a young polar bear become after it is four years old?

Five years old.

Why did the dog
jump into the river?
Because he wanted
to catch a catfish.

What does a frog do
when its car breaks down?
Gets it toad off
and jump-started.

What is the best time
of year for a kangeroo?
A leap year.

What's brown and
sounds like a bell?
Dung.

What's red and flies and wobbles at the same time?

A jellycopter.

"Waiter, this soup tastes funny."

"Then why aren't you laughing?"

Where are whales weighed?

At a whale-weigh station.

Why do you need a licence for a husky dog and not for a cat?

Cats can't drive.

Why did the clock get sick?

It was run down.

"Do you have any invisible ink?"
"Certainly sir. What colour?"

"Why have you been telling everyone that I'm an idiot?"
"I'm sorry, I didn't know it was supposed to be a secret."

"This match won't light!"
"That's funny, it did this morning."

What do you call a husky dog in the middle of a muddy road?
A mutt in a rut.

How do you hire
a polar bear?
Put him on stilts.

Why shouldn't you take polar
bears to the zoo?
Because they'd rather
go to the cinema.

What's the fastest vegetable?
The runner bean.

Have you ever hunted bear?
No, but I've been shooting in my shorts.

What's a teddy bear's favourite pasta?
Tagliateddy.

What do you get if you cross a giraffe with a husky dog?
An animal that barks at low flying aircraft.

What did the finger say to the thumb?
"People will say we're in glove!"

What do you get if you cross a Scottish legend and a bad egg?

The Loch Ness Pongster.

What has a bottom at the top?

Your legs.

What is the smelliest city in America?

Phew York.

How do you catch a runaway husky dog?

Hide behind a tree and make a noise like a bone.

"Why are you covered in bruises?"

"I started to walk through a revolving door and I changed my mind."

When is the best time to buy budgies?

When they're going cheap.

What happens when plumbers die?

They go down the drain.

What kind of meat do you give a stupid husky dog?

Chump chops.

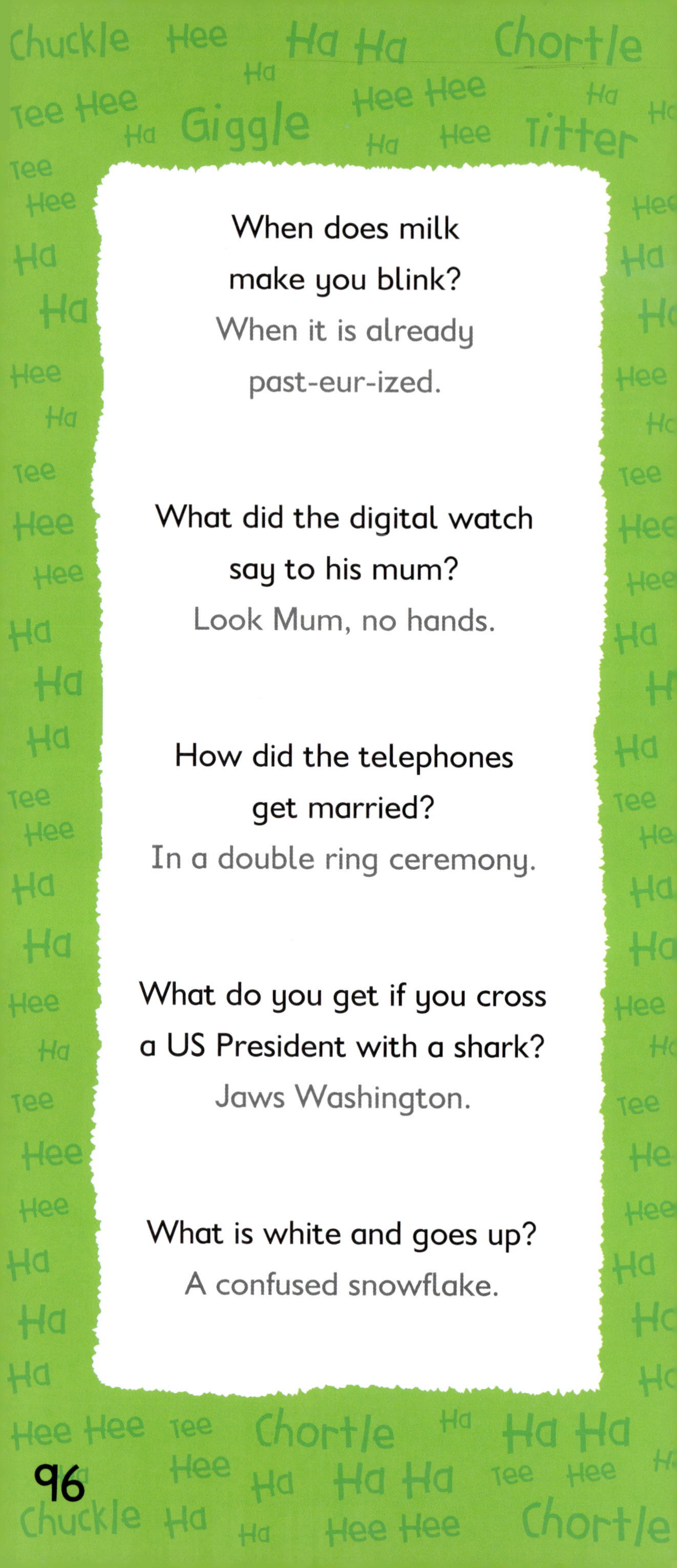

When does milk make you blink?

When it is already past-eur-ized.

What did the digital watch say to his mum?

Look Mum, no hands.

How did the telephones get married?

In a double ring ceremony.

What do you get if you cross a US President with a shark?

Jaws Washington.

What is white and goes up?

A confused snowflake.

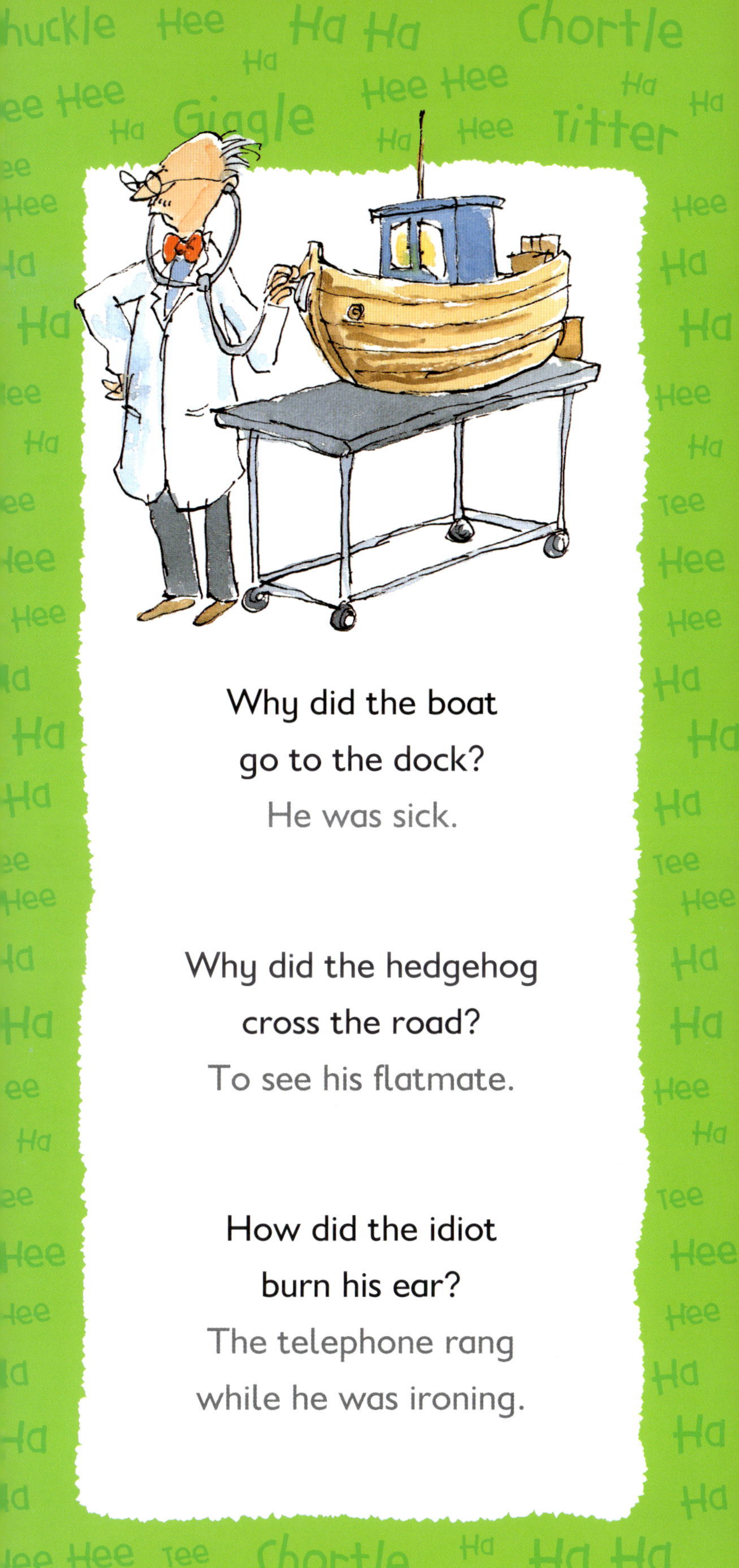

Why did the boat go to the dock?

He was sick.

Why did the hedgehog cross the road?

To see his flatmate.

How did the idiot burn his ear?

The telephone rang while he was ironing.

Super Cool

What's worse than raining cats and dogs?

Hailing taxis.

What's the most popular wine at Christmas?

"But Mum, I don't like sprouts . . ."

Why was Santa's little helper depressed?

Because he had low elf-esteem.

What kind of fish is useful in freezing weather?

Skate.

Why did the sword-swallower swallow an umbrella?

He wanted to put something away for a rainy day.

How do you cure a headache?

Put your head through a window and the pane will just disappear.

What cheese is made backwards?

Edam.

"Have you ever seen a duchess?"

"Yes — it's the same as an English 's'."

Did you hear about the scientist who invented an acid that could burn through anything?

Now he's trying to invent something to keep it in.

What do you get if you cross a husky dog with a blind mole?

A dog that keeps barking up the wrong tree.

What did the fireman's wife get for Christmas?

A ladder in her stocking.

What goes ho-ho-swoosh, ho-ho-swoosh?
Father Christmas caught in a revolving door.

Why does Scrooge live with Rudolph the Reindeer?
Because every buck is dear to him.

What's cold, evil and lives in a candle?
The wicked wick of the north.

What's white and zooms through the snow at 100 mph?
An E-type polar bear.

Have you ever heard
of the tenth reindeer, Olive?
She's in the song —
"Olive the other
reindeer used to laugh
and call him names".

What do you call a cat
at the beach?
Sandy Claws.

What beats his chest and
swings from Christmas cake
to Christmas cake?
Tarzipan.

What can you hold
without touching it?
A conversation.

What did the arctic fishermen sing when they got their Christmas dinner?

"Whalemeat again,
don't know where,
don't know when."

What did the big cracker say to the little cracker?

"My pop is bigger than yours."

Who is never hungry at Christmas?

The turkey — he's always stuffed.

What happened to the paperboy?

He got blown away.

What happens if you eat Christmas decorations?

You get tinsel-itus.

What do vampires put on their turkey at Christmas?

Grave-y.

How do you tell the difference between tinned turkey and tinned custard?

Look at the labels.

What's stupid and yellow?

Thick custard.

What do cannibals eat at tea parties?

Chocolate fingers.

Why do idiots eat biscuits?
Because they're crackers.

What cake wanted
to rule the world?
Attila the Bun.

Where does a general
keep his armies?
Up his sleevies.

What's wet, black
and jumps out of the sea
shouting "Knickers!"?
Crude oil.

What do you call an
American drawing?
Yankee doodle.

What were the gangster's last words?

"Who put that violin in my violin case?"

Why did the burglar take a shower?

He wanted to make a clean getaway.

How long should
a reindeer's legs be?
Just long enough
to reach the ground.

Why did the reindeer wear
sunglasses at the beach?
Because he didn't want
to be recognized.

Why did the reindeer
wear black boots?
Because his
brown ones
were all muddy.

Where do you find reindeer?
It depends on where
you leave them.

What animal carries
an umbrella?
A rain-deer.

What do reindeer have that
no other animals have?
Baby reindeer.

What do you call an
astronaut's watch?
A luna-tic.

Where do little fish
go every morning?
To plaice school.

How many legs does
a reindeer have?
Six. Forelegs at the front
and two at the back.

What's the difference
between a biscuit
and a reindeer?
You can't dunk a reindeer
in your tea.

When should you feed
reindeer milk to a baby?
When it's a baby reindeer.

What lives in the ocean,
is grouchy and hates
neighbours?
A hermit crab.

What's black and white and hums?

A dead penguin.

Why do reindeer scratch themselves?

Because they're the only ones who know where they itch.

What did the dog say to the reindeer?

"Woof, woof."

What do you get from a bad-tempered shark?

As far as away as possible.

Why was the Egyptian girl worried?
Because her daddy was a mummy.

How old is your grandad?
I don't know but we've had him a long time.

"Dad, there is a man at the door collecting for the new swimming pool."
"Give him a glass of water."

What do you get if you cross two young husky dogs with a pair of headphones?
Hush puppies.

What did one virus
say to another?

"Stay away! I think
I've got penicillin."

"Eat up your spinach, it'll
put colour in your cheeks."

"But I don't want
green cheeks."

What is the wettest animal?

A rain-deer.

What do you call a deer with no eyes?

No idea. (No eye deer)

What do you call a deer with no legs and no eyes?

Still no idea.

Why did the whale cross the road?

To get to the other tide.

What do you call a husky dog with no legs?

It doesn't matter what you call him, he still won't come.

What did Mrs Santa say when her husband asked her about the weather?
"Looks like rain, dear."

What do you get if you cross Father Christmas with a detective?
Santa Clues.

Father Christmas won a saucepan in a competition.
Now that's what you call pot luck.

What do you call a big fish who makes you an offer you can't refuse?
The Codfather.

What's wet, black and jumps out of the sea shouting "Underpants!"?

Refined oil.

Why did the stupid racing driver make ten pit stops during the race?

He was asking for directions.

What illness did everyone on the Starship Enterprise catch?

Chicken Spocks.

What is green and has four legs and two trunks?

Two seasick tourists.

Why is perfume obedient?

Because it is scent wherever it goes.

When does a husky dog say “Moo!”?

When it is learning a new language.

What do you call a man
who claps at Christmas?
Santapplause.

Twinkle, twinkle
Chocolate bar,
Santa drives a rusty car,
Press the starter,
Press the choke,
Off he goes in a cloud
Of smoke!

What did one angel
say to the other?
"Halo there."

What happened
to the shark who swallowed
a bunch of keys?
He got lockjaw.

What's Father Christmas called when he takes a rest from delivering presents?

Santa Pause.

Who delivers presents to baby sharks at Christmas?

Santa Jaws.

Why does Santa's sled get such good mileage?

Because there are long-distance runners on each side.

What do Santa's helpers use for cooking?

Elf-raising flour.

What will happen to you at Christmas?

Yule be happy.

What is the best thing to put around a Christmas pudding?

Your mouth.

Why shouldn't you eat reindeer steaks on an empty stomach?

You should eat them on a plate.

How do cats greet each other at Christmas?
"A furry merry Christmas and happy mew year."

What does Dracula write on his Christmas cards?
"Best vicious of the season."

What do angry mice send to each other at Christmas?
Cross mouse cards.

How do we know that Joan of Arc was French?
She was maid in France.

What would happen
if pigs could fly?
Bacon would go up.

How do you close an
envelope underwater?
With a seal.

Why do husky dogs
run in circles?
It's hard to run in squares.

What do you get if you
cross a husky dog
with a kangaroo?
A dog that has somewhere
to put its own lead.

Where do cats like to go on holiday?
The Canary Islands.

What city cheats at exams?
Peking.

Why do giraffes have long necks?
Because they have smelly feet.

How do sheep greet each other at Christmas?
"A merry Christmas to ewe."

What do snowmen wear on their heads?
Ice caps.

How do snowmen travel around?
By icicle.

What do you get if you cross an abbot with a trout?
Monkfish.

What is a horse's favourite cartoon character?
Whinney the Pooh.

What sort of ball
doesn't bounce?
A snowball.

How do you know
when there's a snowman
in your bed?
You wake up wet.

What do you get if you cross
a snowman and a shark?
Frost bite.

What is dry on the outside,
filled with water and
blows up buildings?
A fish tank.

How much do chickens pay
for their trainers?
A poultry amount.

What did the duck say to the
comedian after the show?
"You really quacked me up."

Why are fish boots the
warmest ones to wear?
They have electric eels.

Why are some fish at the bottom of the ocean?

Because they dropped out of their school.

Why did the farmer take hay to bed?

He wanted to feed his nightmares.

What is a dog's favourite snack?

Pupcorn.

What happens when sharks take their clothes off?

They go sharkers.